Accused of a Crime in Maryland?

(Useful Information Revealed That May Help You Defend Your Charges)

By Andrew D. Alpert, Esq.

ISBN: 978-1-941645-03-1

Design and Published by:

Speakeasy Marketing, Inc.
73-03 Bell Blvd #10
Oakland Gardens, NY 11364

www.SpeakeasyMarketingInc.com

888-225-8594

DISCLAIMER

This publication is intended to be informational only. No legal advice is being given, and no attorney-client relationship is intended to be created by reading this material. If you are facing legal issues, whether criminal or civil, seek professional legal counsel to get your questions answered.

Alpert Schreyer, LLC

16901 Melford Boulevard, Ste 325

Bowie, Maryland 20715

(301) 262-7005

www.AndrewAlpert.com

Client Testimonials

"You are an outstanding attorney! I cannot thank you enough for the exceptional work you did handling my case. I am very grateful for your professionalism, depth of knowledge, attention to detail and genuine concern to see that my trial concluded successfully. You saved my life from potentially devastating consequences. Without a doubt, I will recommend you with the highest regard to family and friends."-- **K.H.**

....

"I have never been so impressed with an attorney's desire to fight all the way to insure that I could stay at home with my family and not just be content with what a State's Attorney would offer........If you don't choose wisely, you lose!! And I'm glad I came across the winning team. Thanks Andy." – **L.F.**

....

"...I debated whether to hire a lawyer or not, but consider myself extremely fortunate to have found this firm on the web. After talking to Andy Alpert for only 10 minutes, I knew I wanted him to represent me. I have found him, and his firm, to be not only exceedingly thorough and professional but also to be totally supportive of someone going through what can only be described as "stressful" times. They are "good" people. The ultimate resolution of my case has been excellent, far better than I could have imagined. I couldn't recommend anyone more highly."-- **J.S.**

"My experience with Andrew Alpert was incredible. He represented me with such professionalism and had a true concern for a most favorable outcome. He was extremely skillful and knowledgeable about the law and handled everything without bothering me with the details. At the trial he simply went to the business of getting the best results the he knew possible with precision and confidence......... As a result of his knowledge of the law and his bold skill my case was dismissed and I was able to keep my driver's license. In a word I would say Mr. Alpert is a phenomenal attorney. I would highly recommend him to anyone facing a DUI, DWI or any criminal charge. He's the best one could ever hope for." -- **M.B.**

....

"The best decision I made following my DUI arrest was to hire Andrew Alpert as my attorney. I cannot thank him enough for his exceptional work handling my case. I was definitely facing jail time, but through his efforts the DUI charges were ultimately dropped. For anybody needing a DUI attorney, Mr. Alpert should be at the top of the list." -- **R.L.**

....

"I just wanted to thank you for the excellent job that you did handling my case. Thinking fast on your feet the day of my hearing really made the difference. I would most certainly recommend your services to friends and family. Honestly, thank you." – **P.S.**

....

Past performance does not guarantee future results. Individual results may vary based upon the merits of each case.

TABLE OF CONTENTS

ATTORNEY INTRODUCTION

Attorney Andrew D. Alpert is a Partner with the law firm of Alpert Schreyer, LLC and one of the leading Criminal Defense, (including DUI) attorneys in the state of Maryland and the District of Columbia. A former prosecutor, Mr. Alpert has specific training in DUI/DWI law and has earned a reputation as a highly-skilled and aggressive criminal defense attorney.

He has successfully defended numerous DUI/DWI and motor vehicle manslaughter cases, has had many cases covered by the press (Maryland Independent 09/17/2004 and Maryland Independent 09/22/2004) and has appeared on national television to offer his legal opinion on high-profile criminal cases.

Mr. Alpert regularly attends the National College for DUI Defense, as conducted at Harvard University where he receives yearly advanced training in DUI/DWI defense law.

He is a member of Board of Directors of the Maryland Criminal Defense Lawyer's Association, Chairman of the Legislative Group of the Maryland Criminal Defense

Lawyer's Association on Narcotics, the Maryland State Representative of the National College for DUI Defense and is a member of the Maryland Association for Justice, Maryland State Bar Association, the National Association of Criminal Defense Lawyers, The National Trial Lawyers, The American Trial Lawyers Association, the American Bar Association and The Society of Legal Advocates. He has been named to Super Lawyers in Maryland and the District of Columbia and carries the highest rating available from Martindale-Hubbell (AV® Preeminent).

A graduate of George Washington University School of Law, Alpert is one of only a few lawyers in the state of Maryland and the District of Columbia who is a Certified NHTSA Standardized Field Sobriety Test Instructor.

MISCONCEPTIONS ABOUT BEING CHARGED WITH A CRIME

Interviewer: What are the top misconceptions people have about what is happening to them once they have been arrested for a crime?

Andrew: Let's break it down this way. Assume we are talking about DUI. A top misconception is that those cases cannot be won. That is absolutely false. These cases can be won. But it is better to have your case handled by someone who has training, knowledge and experience; beyond that of just simply being a lawyer.

The public often does not understand the process and the training and experience necessary to effectively cross-examine witnesses for the state, such as police officers and any technical witnesses presented.

They feel they blew into an instrument and therefore they are guilty; or they failed the field sobriety exercises. The bottom line is that almost everyone who comes to me has failed a field sobriety exercise, according to the police officer.

That does not mean they actually failed them, that they did not do okay on them, that their videotape does not look good or that there is no sub-defense available to them. There are lots and lots of sub-defenses.

Quite frankly, just trying cases sometimes generates defenses that you would never expect in the middle of a case. For example, the prosecutor does not have a handle of the evidence or the judge does not like the case for any particular reason.

A lot of people give up too easily and may not even seek a lawyer.

I find that people give up too easily. The reason they give up too easily is because some lawyers out there tell them there is nothing they can do for them.

Interviewer: With general criminal cases, what are people confused about when they come to see you? Are they confused about their Miranda rights?

Andrew: When I handle general criminal cases, people say, "He didn't advise me of my rights." I say, "Well, that may not make a difference at all."

People do not understand that. They say, "Well, I was not advised of my rights. I watch a lot of television and all those cases get thrown out. "Well maybe the statement they gave gets thrown out. But the case does not go away. That is a common misconception.

Another issue arises when people hear what the maximum penalty is. The misconception is they think maybe they are going to get the maximum penalty. Well, that is not anywhere near the truth of it, at all. It really depends on what kind of lawyer you have.

What Are The Advantages Of Hiring A Private Attorney, Instead of A Public Defender?

Interviewer: How do public defenders compare to private attorneys?

Andrew: I am going to be politically correct answering this question. I think there are a lot of really great public defenders out there. Public defenders are lawyers. They go through the same type of training. They go to law school. They have to pass the bar. That is simply where it stops at that point.

We are all lawyers. We all have law degrees. Public defenders, unfortunately, are typically overworked and sometimes underpaid. As a result, while they can be tremendous lawyers, sometimes they cannot give the proper time and attention to cases. Sometimes they just can't spend the time with you that you think is appropriate for representation.

I see this a lot in district court in the state of Maryland because the public defenders have such a high volume of cases that they oftentimes can only speak to their clients the day of a case.

Many have not met their clients until the day of a case. Oftentimes, that is a very difficult scenario for people because they do not have a real opportunity to interact with their lawyer and get comfortable with the person.

Plus, when you apply for and get a public defender, you do not have a right to choose your own lawyer. You are assigned a public defender. If you do not like that particular public defender, you do not have a right to ask to be assigned to a different public defender.

I think public defenders perform a needed service. There are many people who cannot afford lawyers. They need to have representation. Issues arise really as a result of the system and the nature of the case loads; and what we are asking public defenders to do these days.

If you can afford a private attorney, oftentimes you get yourself someone who is much more interested and pays more attention to your case. He or she can give you the time and attention you need for your case.

That is why I recommend that people who can afford to hire a lawyer go ahead and hire that lawyer. If you hire a lawyer, you better make sure that lawyer is a good lawyer. This is because there are a lot of private lawyers out there who try to charge small fees and then not do anything more on the case; potentially even less than a public defender would do on the case. That is the other side of the coin.

Interviewer: When it comes to attorneys, do you get what you pay for?

Andrew: 100% of the time you get what you pay for. Lawyers only have so much time. They can only handle so many cases. The good lawyers out there are busy. The good lawyers out there are in court. They are in court hopefully on a daily basis, for at least a portion of the day. Lawyers who are actively trying cases are the lawyers you should to seek out.

The lawyers who really have a lot of business are the ones who have a lot of time and experience in the saddle. They have the trial experience. They know which cases to try, which cases not to try. That is the important thing.

What to do if you believe you've been 'over-charged'?

Interviewer: Do you find people are maybe overcharged in the beginning? Can you reduce or eliminate some of the charges a person is facing?

Andrew: Yes. The theory, since we were young prosecutors, is basically to charge as much as you possibly can to create what are called throwaways. Police officers in the state of Maryland, who are responsible for charging in misdemeanor cases, often way overcharge.

However, a lot of charges are either thrown out, or nolle prossed or dismissed. This is because they are just not appropriate or they do not match up with the evidence in the case.

Also, a lot of times prosecutors will over indict cases to try to gain leverage. Sometimes, it is not very effective. The answer is, yes, you can reduce the cases significantly and drastically.

Interviewer: I wonder if people easily give up because they are charged with maybe all kinds of counts. They do not even know how it happened and they are afraid they will get the max.

Andrew: That is correct. That is why it is so important to go to a lawyer who has the training and experience to be in a unique position to do things for the client that other lawyers may not be capable of doing. I keep saying that as a theme, but it is really what I believe.

I believe the lawyers who have taken the time to become truly educated in their area of focus and/or concentration are the ones who will be able to do the most in a lot of cases. However, there are very few of these people in the state of Maryland.

Now, this may not apply to all cases. Quite frankly, sometimes there are cases that you just have to simply do the best you can for someone and mitigate their damages as much as possible.

There are a lot of cases where it really truly makes a difference. It is just very difficult to convey that to the client. I tell people, "When you choose a lawyer, you need to be cognizant of what type of training and experience they have. Naturally, it is going to come down to their reputation, their training and experience. Do you feel confident with this person?"

If that in fact is the case, then you have chosen someone good to represent you. Then you just sit back and listen to what they have to say because you are paying them probably a lot of money to assist you. You have to be cooperative and get them all the materials they need to do their job.

Choosing The Right Lawyer To Represent You

Interviewer: Suppose someone has never been in trouble with the law and they do not know the attorney world. How do they know what qualifications and training differentiates lawyers?

Andrew: Here is an example. If you are charged with a DUI, you should want to find out what training and experience an attorney has. Number one, do they handle a lot of DUI cases? Number two, what feedback is there about this particular lawyer?

In other words, when looking at testimonials, you can get a sense of what is a real testimonial, what is probably made up or not that real by the nature of the testimonial.

I recommend reading the testimonials and then going on the website and looking at the experience they have in terms of training. What types of classes have they attended? How many continuing legal education programs do they attend on a yearly basis? What courses have they completed?

Are they a member of the National College of DUI Defense? That is a good indicator of someone who has a lot of training and experience; and who actively attends a lot of training seminars. You need to look at what awards they have received.

How involved are they as a criminal defense lawyer across the state of Maryland? How many cases do they handle on a yearly basis in that area? Quite frankly, repetition does make for a better lawyer. If someone is extremely busy that means they are probably doing something very right.

You want someone who has training in standardized field sobriety testing. You want someone better, an instructor in standardized field sobriety testing. Frankly, there are only two of us that I know in the state of Maryland who are instructors.

You want to find someone trained in forensics and in the Breathalyzer and various instruments. You want to find someone trained in forensic drug analysis, gas chromatography.

You want someone who has taken lots of classes in scientific evidence. DUI cases are a blend of science, as well as simply eyewitness testimony.

How Experience As A Prosecutor Can Make For A More Skilled Criminal Defense Attorney

Interviewer: You were a prosecutor for five years and participated in 150 plus jury trials. That is huge. What other factors helped you become a better criminal defense lawyer?

Andrew: When you are a former prosecutor, you gain a unique perspective. You understand what is going through the prosecutor's head as they are thinking about a case.

I now understand where the pressure points are for prosecutors. It is important to understand how a prosecutor thinks, what their agenda is and what is important to them.

Then as a defense lawyer, you can come in and apply pressure at the right moment and the right time. This tactic will get your client much better dispositions in my opinion, than other lawyers who have not had that experience.

They just do not know what that person is going through. They have not experienced what it is like to be a prosecutor. They are unaware of the various issues prosecutors have to deal with and what is important to them.

You can also help prepare your clients better for coming into court. Let me give you an example using clients charged with DUI offenses or sometimes, let's say drug offenses. They will take a drug education or alcohol education class regardless of whether I think I can achieve a victory for them. I want them to do that so I have that in my back pocket when I go in.

I can negotiate with the prosecutor and say, "This case is really not worthy of prosecution. My client has already completed a program. I am going to give you that certificate of completion. You can put it in your file."

You can rest assure that even though you dismissed 90% or 100% of the charges, at least you can go back to your office and tell your supervisor you got rid of this case but this person did this program." That helps me negotiate a lot of cases. There are a lot of different ways to do things.

How Much Information Should You Give The Police?

Interviewer: What common mistakes do people make once they have been arrested that unintentionally makes their case worse?

Andrew: That is talking. The biggest mistake you can make is to keep talking to the police about your case. People think they can talk themselves out of charges. I see it worst in the beginning. Someone gets stopped by a police officer and thinks they can talk their way out of the case. Again, talking may be the worst thing you do.

Quite frankly, I do not believe people should do field sobriety exercises. In the state of Maryland, there is no requirement to take field sobriety exercises. So why would you? Yes, maybe you will get arrested; but the bottom line is you just deprived the state of a lot of evidence against you.

When you are overly talkative, for instance in a DUI case, you allow the cop to hear what you sound like. You are interacting too much. You are saying too much to the police and they are recording it or writing it down. That is the problem people have. They interact too much.

Then there is a cathartic process they go through at the station. They start to try to tell the police officer they are sorry they did something. That does not help you either. When you go through that desire to confess to make yourself feel better, all you are doing is providing evidence to the prosecutorial team.

Interviewer: Do the police lie to you? Are they allowed to lie to you?

Andrew: The police absolutely are allowed to lie to people. In fact, they often lie when they are interrogating people. The most typical lie police tell occurs if you are involved in a case with a codefendant.

They separate you two and say, "Your codefendant just gave you up. He said this and this." That causes you to become upset. Then you get angry at your codefendant and say something bad about your codefendant; when in fact that may not have been true.

Police are actually allowed to lie. There is no punishment for them for lying. It is a common method of interrogation that they use. Unfortunately, the problem is the public just does not understand their rights.

It is important to educate people on their rights. Frankly, I have had a lot of success with that. I've had people who know what their rights are. They've told police officers, "I know what my rights are. I do not want to talk to you anymore;" or "I am not going to do what you ask me to do." Sometimes those cases just go away because there is no evidence against them.

Interviewer: Once a case is ongoing, do people talk about their case, perhaps using social media? How does talking about your case with friends and family create problems?

Andrew: If you come to us, we advise that you absolutely not speak to anyone about your case. Let me give you an example, one that is fairly obvious.

Suppose we have to come visit you in a jail somewhere because you have been charged with an offense and you are still incarcerated. You do not want to talk to your cellmate about what happened because those people are trying to create favor with the prosecutors.

They may say, "Knock, knock. I have some information I want to provide to you about my cellmate." They may want to curry favor with the prosecutor. The prosecutor says, "Sure, I'll make a deal with you. Tell me what he said." Then all of a sudden, you've created a witness. That is a real obvious situation.

The less obvious is when you go on a website, perhaps Facebook, and you start to provide information. In a prosecution, especially if you will take the witness stand and testify, all that stuff can be used against you. If you brag about doing something, that can be used against you also.

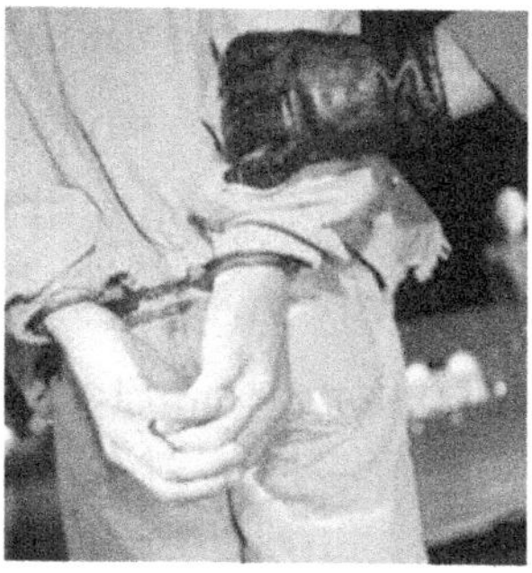

You really do not want to talk to anybody. That includes your friends and your family, and I tell people blame me. Suppose you are a kid and your parents come with you to an interview. I say to the parents, "Look, your child is of age. If he does not want you in the room, I think it is a good idea that you sit out."

I get better information that way. Kids are less concerned about what their parents think when talking to the lawyer by themselves. Then they do not create witnesses.

How To Find Out About The Charges Against You

Interviewer: When someone is charged with a crime, how public will their situation be? Will friends and families find out?

Andrew: It depends on the nature of the case, obviously. If a case does attract a lot of publicity, there is not much you will be able to do. If the press does call you, I instruct all my clients to say no comment; or say, "I am represented. You will have to talk to my lawyer." Then my office handles all the inquiries.

We generally have a policy here at the office that we do not comment during pending cases because quite frankly, it creates more problems than not. As far as smaller cases, the charges are going to be logged into the system now. With computers, everyone has access to the Maryland Criminal Justice System and they can find out what you have been charged with.

Some newspapers will publish arrests of people. That may get out to the public. For the average case, there probably isn't much you have to worry about in terms of a lot of people finding out about it.

The more important problem is for people who have security clearances and jobs where they are required to tell their superiors if they've been charged or have criminal charges pending against them. Then, obviously, it becomes quite public at that point in time.

Can A Guilty Person Be Found Not Guilty?

Interviewer: How often do people say, "You know what? I did it. I am guilty. Maybe I should just give up and throw myself on the mercy of the court." What do you say to those people?

Andrew: I say, "That's great and that's nice. Maybe in fact we will have to say that in your particular case. Although I will control what you say and I will help craft what you say to the court. Also, I will control and suggest what mitigation you do in order to present yourself in the most favorable manner to the court." That is my job as an attorney.

I tell people, "Honestly, that is really not my concern. My concern is the proof against you. Does the state of Maryland have proof? Can they prove it beyond a reasonable doubt? When it comes to your guilt or your innocence, I want you to be found not guilty." That is different from being innocent.

Oftentimes, a not guilty finding is another way of saying not proven beyond the reasonable doubt. In other words, the government, the state of Maryland has not proven their case. That is just as good. It does not mean you are innocent of the charges. It just means that they do not have the proof to do that. That is what this is all about.

Interviewer: Does it help a case if people say, "You know, I am not that kind of person. I have a family. I attend church. I do this and that." Will authorities see that and just drop a case?"

Andrew: Here's what I say: There are times when your background and who you are as a person will make a difference in terms of convincing a prosecutor to sometimes not prosecute a case. It depends. Everyone charged with a crime has a different background. It depends on the nature of the crime, how serious it is and your background.

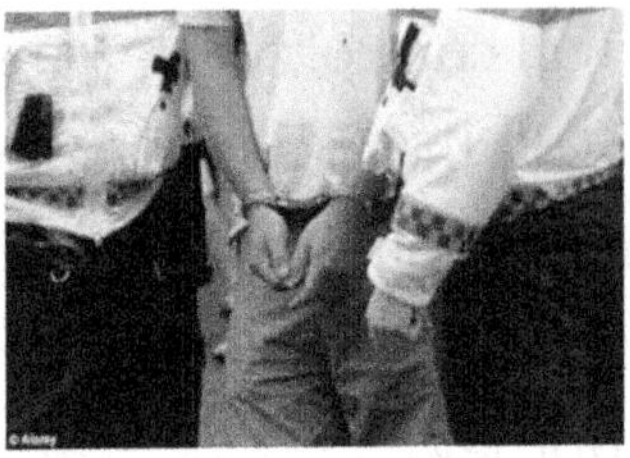

Through thorough investigation of your background and talking with you during the intake process, I learn a lot about you. There may be something in your background that is worthy of bringing to the attention of the prosecutor, to see if the prosecutor will consider not prosecuting you.

Unfortunately, that happens pretty rarely because prosecutors have pretty much seen a lot of different people get charged with crimes. It is not necessarily going to help you but it could be a factor.

What To Do If The Police Want To Speak To You Regarding A Criminal Matter

Interviewer: Besides being arrested obviously, how does someone know they are under criminal investigation? Suppose you get a call from a detective or the police and they say, "We want to talk to you." What does that mean?

Andrew: There are a lot of different ways to know that you are under investigation. Sometimes in the federal system, you get a letter saying that you are the target of an investigation.

That does not happen in the state system. In the state system, oftentimes you will simply just receive a telephone call saying, "I am Detective So and So and I'd like to ask you some questions about something that happened. Can you come to the station and talk to me?"

That is a red flag. That red flag should go up and you should absolutely contact an attorney and talk to an attorney. It is not wise to simply try to do it over the phone. You should consider meeting with a lawyer.

You need to provide as much information and disclosure to a lawyer as possible; regarding what you know about the facts and circumstances that they are going to ask you about.

You may want to bring a lawyer with you to a meeting with the police. You may have the lawyer intercede on your behalf and talk to the police. The lawyer may tell the police, "No, we are not going to provide a statement at this time."

You may want your lawyer to ask, "What questions are going to be asked? What information are you looking for? What authority do you have to make any deals with my client if my client has information that helps you?" There are a lot of scenarios.

Most important, if you are ever contacted by someone, do not think you can handle it on your own because it is not a wise decision. It is very easy to make mistakes. You will think one thing and they will ask you questions about something else.

They can lie to you. They can say, "We're going to ask you questions about something that happened on September 12th." Then you get in there and they say, "By the way, we want to ask you about what happened in March."

You just do not know what happens psychologically. You are under the pressure of that inquisition or questioning, and you do not think clearly. You cannot think through all of the ramifications of what you are doing.

That is the reason you absolutely need counsel. Do not expect to call a lawyer and say, "I just need to ask you a quick question and get the answer over the phone." Do not expect that is good advice that you can take to the bank and handle matters yourself. You can't.

Interviewer: If the police or a detective calls you, how do you tell them in a nice way that you want to speak to a lawyer first? Will they come arrest you?

Andrew: They may come and arrest you either way. I tell clients, "You have to be polite. You have to try to be calm." You have to say, "Upon the advice of counsel, I cannot talk to you at this time. If you want to talk to me, you have to contact my counsel."

Unfortunately, you may or may not get arrested. But, again, that may happen either way. This way, if you get arrested you have already invoked your right to counsel and they can't talk to you.

Let's say I am a cop and I call and say I want to talk to you. You say, "Upon the advice of counsel, I can't speak to you." If you are picked up later and they try to ask you questions again, you have already invoked your right to counsel. I think it would be illegal for them to try to ask you further questions. That is why it is really important.

It is important to talk to a lawyer because a lawyer will give you this advice: When you go to that station or get transported by that police officer who starts to make pleasant chitchat with you in the car, you need to keep your mouth shut. Spontaneous statements by a person can be used against them.

Suppose you are arrested and for whatever reason you just feel like talking about whatever it is that you did. If the police officer is not asking you questions, they can use all that evidence against you.

He's just driving in the car. Meanwhile, you start talking about whatever it is that may or may not have happened because you want to get it off your chest. That is just going to get you into more trouble.

Interviewer: Do people talk because it makes them feel better?

Andrew: Absolutely. It is human nature. That is why it is so important to be able to say, "I would really love to talk to you but my lawyer has told me that I cannot talk to you." That way you blame it on the lawyer and that is the end of it.

Different Ways You Can Be Charged With A Crime

Interviewer: You mentioned indictment a couple of times. How does an indictment differ from just a regular criminal charge?

Andrew: There are all types of criminal charges. Let me explain: In the state of Maryland, when you get a speeding ticket that is a criminal citation. You can get

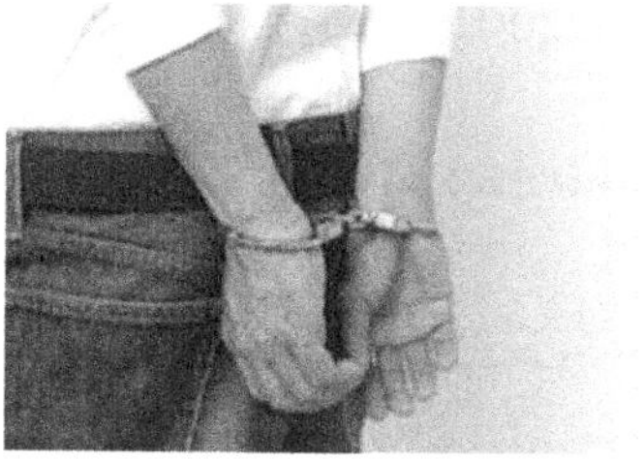

criminal citations for a lot of different types of crimes. They are mostly misdemeanors and they can be handed to you by the police. All traffic offenses and some small drug offenses can be charged by citation. That is one type of a charging document.

A second type of a charging document is called information. That is simply a fancy word for a written piece of paper charging you with a crime. That can be done in certain circumstances by the prosecutors in the state of Maryland.

The third type of charge is called an indictment. An indictment is another fancy word meaning the grand jury in a county in which the incident may have occurred got together and returned a charging document against you. That is what an indictment is. It alleges all the various things you are charged with doing.

Those are the three different ways you can be charged with crimes.

Interviewer: So there are just different ways you can be charged.

Andrew: That is correct.

IF ARRESTED, HOW DO YOU MAKE BAIL & DO YOU QUALIFY?

Interviewer: How does the bail system work? When arrested, how much will bail be for various offenses? How do you pay?

Andrew: The bail system can be very complicated. There are various types. In Maryland, if you get arrested police officers, depending upon the type of charge, have discretion as to whether or not they want to simply just release you on a citation. They can do that.

For example, if you have a small amount of marijuana or cocaine in your purse, they can charge you via citation.

They can hand you a citation and release you from the station. Then you do not have to worry about bail. There is no bail because you have been released.

The other way is to file a charging document against you and bring you before a district court commissioner. The commissioner, also known as the old justice of the peace, is the first level of the judiciary in the state of Maryland. Commissioners are not judges, but they are authorized to make bail determinations.

The commissioner will look at the charges and determine whether there is probable cause. In other words, the commissioner determines if there is a 51% chance based on the allegations that you are the person who committed this alleged crime; and if the facts of what the police officer says occurred match up with the elements of the crime. If they determine there is probable cause, then they can set a bail.

Typically the way they determine bail is they evaluate the case: the seriousness of the case, whether or not you are dangerous, whether or not you have prior criminal offenses, whether those prior criminal offenses have been dismissed or prosecuted; and whether or not you have a history with court and, if so, do you appear for trial.

Basically they use their best judgment to determine what the bond or the bail should be, based on the circumstances. They can set it a number of different ways. Typically, they set a surety bond. That means you can go out and hire a bail bondsman who can post bail for you.

Your fee to the bail bondsman is about 10% of the total bail. So if you have a $1,000 bond and you want to get out, you might have to provide $100 to the bail bondsman. That is their fee. You do not get that $100 back. That $100 is gone but you will be able to get out. If you fail to appear, then technically the bondsman is responsible for bringing you in to the court system.

There can also be other types of bond. For instance, you can pay 10% to the court. In other words, if you have a case and it is a $10,000 bond, you can pay $1,000 to the court. You can get out. If you show up for court, you get your $1,000 back.

There are different nuances on the scheme, but that is essentially the nature of the bond system in the state of Maryland.

Following Your Arrest, What Is The Court Process? How Long Will It Take To Resolve Your Case?

Interviewer: When a person is arrested and formally charged, what is the typical process regarding your case? What happens and what is the timeframe?

Andrew: It really depends on the nature of the crime. We have to talk about two different scenarios in Maryland.

If you are charged with a crime for which the jurisdiction of the crime is the district court of Maryland, then typically you've either been charged by a citation from a police officer or via information from the prosecutor's office.

The case will be held in the district court which is the lowest court. With the district court in Maryland, those are bench trials. In other words, those are judge trials.

Typically those cases are held within three to four months; maybe sooner depending how busy that particular county is. Urban environments have a lot more cases than rural environments. Rural environments advance faster than urban environments.

You can go to district court in Maryland. If your case carries a maximum penalty of 90 days or more, you theoretically are entitled to a jury trial if you want to avoid the bench trial you are entitled to in the district court.

You can remove that case to the circuit court if you want; sometimes prolonging the case. You get a jury trial or a bench trial in the circuit court if you want one. That is one way cases go.

If you are charged with a crime and the jurisdiction of that crime technically is in the circuit court, like for most felonies, then typically you request a preliminary hearing in the state of Maryland. That preliminary hearing must be held 30 days from the time you are arrested.

During that time period, basically I have to hold a preliminary hearing in a district court. That preliminary hearing is to determine whether there is probable cause this even occurred and you are the person who committed the offense.

If a preliminary hearing is held within 30 days, then the case is bound over to the circuit court. That means it gets referred to the circuit court and the circuit court will charge the case. You can be detained if there is probable cause found.

The other way is you can be charged in the district court. If a probable cause determination is not held and there is a lapse of 30 days, the case theoretically could be dismissed for lack of prosecution.

Most felonies have no statute of limitations in the state of Maryland. You can be charged via an indictment later on. If you get indicted, if the grand jury meets and returns an indictment, you can either get a summons to appear in court or you can be picked up on a warrant.

Then, there is a rule in the circuit court called the speedy trial rule. It is different than your constitutional speedy trial rights. In Maryland, the rule is called the Hicks Rule. It says you have to be actually tried within 180 days from your first presentment in the circuit court.

Interviewer: About how long will it take to resolve a case?

Andrew: If it is a serious case, it can take anywhere from four months to a year. If it is a misdemeanor case, it can take anywhere from two to six months on average.

Interviewer: What is the difference between a misdemeanor charge and a felony charge?

Andrew: Let's talk generalities first. In general, a misdemeanor is typically a charge in Maryland that carries a more lenient sentence than a felony charge. That is the easiest definition.

Unfortunately, there can be misdemeanors in the state of Maryland that carry hefty penalties. For instance, second degree assault is a misdemeanor in Maryland, but it carries a maximum penalty of 10 years in jail.

Possession of marijuana can be a misdemeanor with one year in jail and a $1,000 fine. Possession with the intent to distribute marijuana is a felony charge and it carries a five-year maximum in the state of Maryland.

Typically, it is basically designated by statute but there is a common rule. The common rule is anything that is not determined to be a felony by statute is by operation of law a misdemeanor.

Interviewer: Are you often able to improve someone's situation by getting charges reduced, dismissed or mitigated; so your client ends up better off than they would have been without you?

Andrew: I would say 98% of the time.

Consequences Of Pleading Guilty To A First-Time Criminal Offense

Interviewer: Do people say, "It's my first offense so maybe I'll just let this one go and move on?" What happens if there is a second offense?

Andrew: That is a problem. This is especially a huge problem in the state of Maryland. Maryland has a pretty lenient first offender situation. The court systems are designed to, in my opinion, give first offenders a break so they learn from their mistakes and not repeat the behavior.

The problem I find is a lot of the lawyers suggest to people that they simply just take the deal, plead out or take that first offender status because it is not a big deal. However, they do not realize they are potentially setting people up for heartache down the road.

The problem is you cannot tell who is going to get in trouble again and who is not going to get in trouble again. I try not to analyze cases that way. I try to look at cases and say, "This is the case that needs to be tried or this is a case that needs to be worked out." I tend not to pay attention to what the disposition is going to be on the case. I find that clouds my judgment on whether I should try cases.

Even though you are a first offender I might say to you, "This is a case that you really need to try because I think you can win this case." That way God forbid something should happen again to you, you are considered a first offender; versus simply saying, "Take the deal." Sometimes, take the deal is good advice.

Interviewer: Do you have a look back period, after which you are considered a first time offender again?

Andrew: The answer is no. For example, in the state of Maryland suppose you have a DUI that is a first offense that is not aggravated in some way. It is a plain, benevolent DUI. Chances are you will end up with probation before judgment finding, if you do not win your case. That means you do not receive any points; and technically, under Maryland law that is not considered a conviction.

However, the probation before judgment is stored by the Motor Vehicle Administration as part of your record; although it is only available to law enforcement. The problem is technically after 10 years, you would be eligible for a second probation before judgment. But eligible does not mean you are going to get it.

Most judges will not give you a second probation before judgment. There is no "look back period" that saves you. It is forever.

There have been instances where judges have said, "Mr. So and So, you had a DUI 25 years ago and you got a probation before judgment. I am not going to give you another probation before judgment. This will be a conviction even though the first offense occurred 25 years ago." That is within the discretion of the judge.

Interviewer: So it is important to fight every charge, whether it is your first time or not.

Andrew: Exactly. Not fighting them is the mistake I see lawyers across the state make all the time. Many lawyers feel, "Well, it is a first offense. No big deal. I'll just go in and plea them guilty. I'll get my probation before judgment and we'll walk out the door. Everything will be fine."

There are a lot of cases out there that should be tried on the facts. However, they are not getting tried because either the lawyer doesn't know how to try them; or he doesn't have the training and experience necessary to try them. He simply takes the easy way out and accepts a disposition which is seemingly benign at the time.

However, many years later it creates a problem for someone.

Interviewer: Can you ever get something on your record expunged or sealed?

Andrew: Yes, but that is very limited in the state of Maryland. If the case is dismissed, if you are found not guilty, or if the case is nolle prosequi- dismissed by the state of Maryland; then there are provisions which allow you to get your record expunged. Also, if a case is stet, you can get that expunged too.

There are some complications involved. There are time requirements. Sometimes the time requirement is up to three years, depending on the circumstances. Sometimes it isn't, if you sign a waiver allowing the expungement to go forward. But you waive your right to sue police officers for any misconduct during the arrest.

If you are convicted of an offense in the state of Maryland, you cannot get an expungement of that offense. If you get probation before judgment for an offense, you may be entitled to an expungement of the probation before judgment for criminal offenses.

Interestingly enough, the exception is that you cannot expunge a DUI for which you receive probation before judgment, which is not a conviction. The reason is if we expunge all those DUIs, we would never have a record of prior DUI census.

That is what is happening out there. It is important to fight cases because employers do background checks. Also, schools and other entities check your background when you apply for a job or for student aide. They go to the various databases that are available to them.

Those databases will reveal that you had probation before judgment in the state of Maryland, which is known as a deferred judgment. Now, technically under Maryland law, it is not a conviction. Still, a lot of employers may look at it and say, "No way." That is the reason it is more important to fight now than it ever was before.

Interviewer: Is information about arrests permanent?

Andrew: Arrests without convictions can be expunged almost immediately. You can wipe that off. When you expunge a case in the state of Maryland, you can expunge it from police files, from the commissioner's files, from the prosecutor's files and from court files also.

However, because of 9/11, oftentimes if you have been entered into the NCIS system-the National Criminal Information System- that will not get expunged.

Interviewer: Really; no matter what?

Andrew: Even though there is an order directed to expunge all reference to this alleged crime that took place because you were arrested, and let's say not prosecuted, they are not expunging.

Interviewer: Can you force them?

Andrew: No, it is almost impossible.

Can You Avoid Jail and Other Penalties?

Interviewer: Are you able to get people alternative punishments to jail; such as house arrest, community service or probation?

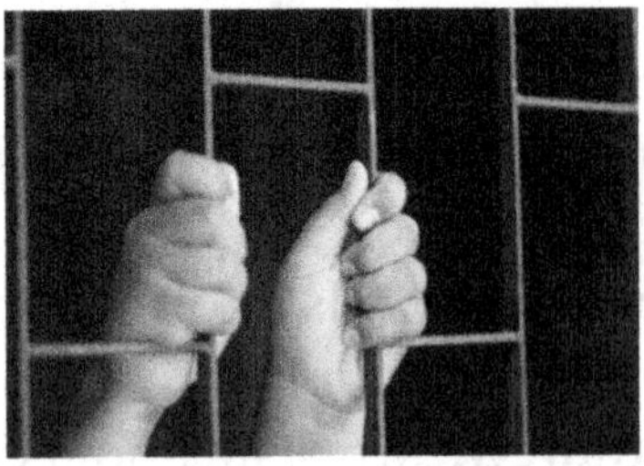

Andrew: That depends on the creativity of your lawyer. He or she has to figure whether alternative sentencing is going to fly with the judge; or make a difference to the prosecutor in terms of having the case dropped or reduced, achieving stet docket or getting probation before judgment.

All mitigations have to be looked upon. I try to look at the case and ask, "What would be a good alternative for my client in the event that something goes terribly wrong at trial?"

Here's where I think I make a huge difference: by frontloading their punishment. When I walk in the court, I go to the prosecutor and say, "Johnny has done 200 hours of community service. Here is a letter documenting that community service." That is a lot of community service. I say I think a way to resolve this matter would be to put this case on a stet docket; good behavior for six months. Then Johnny gets a nolle prossed, or a dismiss, after six months has gone by because he has done all this work upfront. A lot of prosecutors are very amenable to that, especially if there is a tiny issue or problem in their case.

Interviewer: Can you share the story of an interesting case you successfully handled?

Andrew: Sure. I've had a lot of cases but one of the most interesting cases I handled is a motor vehicle manslaughter case in which it was alleged that two motorcycles were racing on the roadway.

A drunk driver pulled out from a bar. One of the motorcycles hit the drunk driver. That motorcycle catapulted 375 yards into the oncoming lane of traffic on the other side of the road. He was run over by a truck.

They charged the other motorcyclist with motor vehicle manslaughter because he was engaged in a race contest;

notwithstanding the fact that there was a drunk driver that pulled out from a bar.

We were able to prove that the state expert, who they were relying upon for various issues, was either lying or terribly mistaken and did not do correct work when reconstructing the accident. Therefore, my client was acquitted of the manslaughter charges.

We did that through the use of science, by doing a tremendous amount of homework and by being able to effectively cross-examine the expert in the trial. That avoided a maximum penalty of 15 years in jail. My client has gone on to have a very successful life.

Interviewer: Why should people contact you regarding their criminal defense case?

Andrew: I have spent my career not only defending people accused of crimes; but also trying to become the best possible advocate. I do this by trying to make myself knowledgeable in trial skills, forensics, forensic science and all aspects of trying cases.

I then take those skills into the courtroom. I try to affect a great outcome. I believe that I possess highly developed skills based on my training and experience that enable me to create great outcomes. I handle cases very differently and I think that is what makes me unique.

DISCLAIMER

This publication is intended to be informational only. No legal advice is being given, and no attorney-client relationship is intended to be created by reading this material. If you are facing legal issues, whether criminal or civil, seek professional legal counsel to get your questions answered.

Alpert Schreyer, LLC
16901 Melford Boulevard, Ste 325
Bowie, Maryland 20715
(301) 262-7005
www.AndrewAlpert.com

Made in the USA
Monee, IL
05 November 2026

67843128R00030